Why Should I Should I
Recycle
Garbage?

M J Knight

PLÁSTICO

LATA

VIDRO

SAUNDERS
BOOK COMPANY

Published by Saunders Book Company
27 Stewart Road
Collingwood, ON Canada L9Y 4M7

Library of Congress Cataloging-in-Publication Data

Knight, M. J. (Mary-Jane)
    Why should I recycle garbage? / M.J. Knight.
    p. cm. — (Smart Apple Media. One small step)
    Summary: "Facts about how recycling can reduce waste and
practical tips for kids about how they can contribute to waste
reduction"—Provided by publisher.
    Includes bibliographical references and index.
    ISBN 978-1-897563-47-2 (pbk)
    1. Recycling (Waste, etc.)—Juvenile literature. I. Title.
TD794.5.K544 2009
363.72'82—dc22

                                                    2008011374

Designed by Guy Callaby
Edited by Jinny Johnson
Illustrations by Hel James
Picture research by Su Alexander

Picture acknowledgements
Title Page Paulo Fridman/Corbis; 4 Stuart McCall/Getty Images;
6 Anne Domdey/Corbis; 7 Michael S. Lewis/Corbis; 9 Gary Bell/
Zefa/Corbis; 10 Louise Murray/Getty Images; 12 Roger Wood/
Corbis; 14 Paulo Fridman/Corbis; 16 Nick Vedros & Assoc./Getty
Images; 19 Lester Lefkowitz/Corbis; 21 Allan H. Shoemake/Getty
Images; 22 James L. Amos/Corbis; 24 Randy Faris/Corbis;
26 Gari Wyn Williams/Alamy; 28 Don Smith/Alamy.
Front cover: Gary Buss/Getty Images

Printed in the United States of America
in North Mankato, Minnesota
072012
DAD0024f

9 8 7 6 5

Contents

A Mountain of Garbage

Every year we throw away more garbage than we did the year before. Americans threw away more than 251 million tons (228 million t) of garbage in 2006.

If we keep throwing away this much garbage, we are going to run out of places to put it. So everyone needs to stop and think about how to make less garbage.

There are twice as many people in the world now as 100 years ago, and we all throw away lots of garbage.

What Is Reusing and Recycling?

One way to make less garbage is to reuse things instead of throwing them away. You can use plastic bags again and again. Recycling is when old items such as glass, plastics, paper, or metal are processed and the materials are used again to make new items. Making new items from recycled items uses less energy than making them from scratch.

A Step in the Right Direction

You might think that what you do doesn't matter, but it does. It matters very much. Every time you recycle a glass jar or use a plastic bag again instead of taking a new one, you take a small step towards making less garbage. You can make a difference—everyone can. And if lots of people take a small step in the right direction, they add up to one big step.

5

That's Garbage!

What do you do when you don't want something any more? You throw it away—it's garbage. Garbage can be anything from a candy wrapper to a broken toy.

At home we throw away leftover food, packaging, paper, cans, and bottles. This is called household waste. The garbage that stores, offices, factories, and schools throw away is called industrial and commercial waste.

About 12 percent of the garbage in our trash cans is food we have thrown away.

Cleaning Up Everest

You would think that Mount Everest, the world's highest mountain, would be a very clean place, with no garbage. But climbers have left lots of junk such as cans, old tents, food, and medicine behind them over the years. Japanese climber Ken Noguchi has been cleaning up Mount Everest. He has made five trips to the peak with some other climbers. They have collected a total of 10 tons (9,000 kg) of garbage!

Garbage Can Be Dangerous

Some trash can harm people, animals, and the world around us. Harmful garbage includes things such as batteries, paint, and electrical equipment. We all need to be very careful about where and how we throw these things away.

Too Much Garbage

American households throw away about 150 million tons (136 million t) of trash per year—more than half a ton for every person! In Canada, households throw away about 14 million tons (13 million t) of garbage per year, but that's still two-fifths of a ton per person.

Lots of things we throw away could be useful to someone else—from furniture to toys.

One Small Fact

The garbage every household throws away each year weighs as much as a teenage elephant!

I Can Make a Difference

Check out your family's garbage. How many bags of garbage did your household throw out this week?

Count how many plastic or glass bottles and cans your family recycles and check how much paper or cardboard your family recycles.

Is there anything else in the garbage that you could reuse or recycle?

A Load of Garbage

The biggest waste dump in the world is floating on the Pacific Ocean. The Great Pacific Garbage Patch is nearly four times the size of Great Britain. Almost all the garbage in the patch is floating plastic.

What Happens to Our Garbage?

Most of the garbage we put out every week is picked up by garbage trucks. They take the garbage to landfills, where it is buried in the ground.

In the United States, more than half of garbage is buried in landfills. The rest is either burned, recycled, or composted. In Canada, about three-quarters of total garbage goes to landfills. Some countries, including Denmark and Sweden, burn more than half of their garbage.

A dump truck empties out a load of garbage in a landfill site near London.

One Small Fact

Everyone throws away their own weight in garbage every seven weeks.

Think about the different kinds of garbage in your trash can. Some, such as paper, food leftovers, and grass clippings, rot away after a while. This kind of garbage is called biodegradable. Other kinds never rot. This type of garbage includes bottles and cans.

Biodegradable

Nonbiodegradable

A Step in the Right Direction

One way to make less garbage is to buy fewer things, or buy things with less packaging. When you help with the shopping, try to find food that does not have lots of wrapping. Look for fruit and vegetables that are sold loose instead of in plastic trays.

Market stalls are great places to buy food that doesn't have a lot of packaging. This stall in a market in Pakistan sells fresh fruits and nuts.

I Can Make a Difference

Do you bring a packed lunch to school? Is the food wrapped in packaging that you throw away? Cut down on the garbage from your packed lunch by bringing it in a plastic box that you can use every day. Ask your mom and dad to buy a reusable bottle for drinks so you don't have drink cartons, cans, or bottles to throw away.

Reuse Grocery Bags

Remind everyone to take cloth bags when you go shopping. You can use them over and over again, so you won't need lots of plastic bags for shopping.

Help your mom and dad by looking for items such as toilet paper rolls and paper towels made from recycled paper. Buying recycled items means that you are using less of the things that are needed to make them.

One Small Fact

In the United States, the average amount of garbage thrown away per person per year hasn't changed much since 1990—about 1,650 lbs (750 kg) per year. But in 1990, only 16% of this was recycled. In 2006, 32.5% of garbage was recycled.

What Can I Recycle?

Think before you throw anything in the trash.
Lots of things can be recycled, such as paper,
plastic and glass bottles, cans, grass clippings,
and much more. Keep a special bin or box next to
the garbage can to help you remember to recycle.

It's easy to recycle when
recycling bins are different
colors and clearly labeled, like
this row of bins in Brazil.

Can I Use These Again?

Look at the pictures and write down on a piece of scrap paper the ones you think can be recycled or reused. Answers on page 32.

Find out the best way to recycle. In some areas you can put recyclables into special boxes or bags that the garbage collectors pick up. They are collected at a different time from the rest of the garbage. Or you can take things for recycling to a center where there are big bins for glass, cans, paper, and other things.

See if you can find any clothes and toys you don't want anymore. Take them to a charity shop so other people can use them. If you have a yard, you can put your yard waste in a special bin. It rots down into a kind of earth called compost and can be put on the soil to help plants grow.

Piles and Piles of Paper

Most of us have so much paper! But there is no need to throw away newspapers, magazines, junk mail, cardboard, or even your old homework. It is easy to recycle most of the paper we use.

Find out if your school has a paper recycling program. If it does, get together with friends and see if you can find out how often the paper is collected and where it goes. If your school doesn't recycle paper yet, ask if you can start.

One Small Fact

Every ton of paper recycled saves 17 trees.

I Can Make a Difference

Keep a box at home for recycled paper. It could be a cardboard box or a special box or bag from the local council. Every time you finish with a comic or a magazine, put it in the box. If you have been using paper for a project, put all the leftover pieces in the box. When the box is full, help your mom and dad take it to a paper recycling bin. Or put it out to be collected on the day your local recycling team comes around.

North Americans use on average more than 660 pounds (300 kg) per person of paper every year. More than half of this is recycled.

How Is Paper Recycled?

The paper we put into recycling bins is sorted and then taken to a place called a paper mill. It is made into pulp and washed. Any staples and glue are taken out. Then the pulp is put into a tank like a giant washing machine where soap removes the ink from the paper.

1. Waste paper is sorted.

2. Sorted paper is pulped.

3. Pulp has the coarse bits filtered out.

4. Pulp is washed, and ink is removed.

5. Clean pulp is dried and rolled into sheets.

I Can Make a Difference

Think about cutting down the amount of paper you use and throw away. Always use both sides of a piece of paper.

Keep a box of scrap paper to use for scribbling notes.

Unwrap presents carefully so that you can use the wrapping paper again. Cut pictures out of cards you are sent or use colorful paper to make your own greeting cards.

The washed paper goes into an enormous machine. The machine squeezes the water out between two wire meshes and winds the dry paper onto enormous reels. The reels are sent to printers to be turned into new newspapers and magazines.

Each of these huge reels of paper weighs several tons.

New Paper from Old

● About half of everything we put out for recycling is paper and cardboard.

● A paper recycling machine makes 1.2 miles (2 km) of paper a minute.

● Old newspapers and magazines can be recycled into new ones in only seven days.

Can I Recycle Metal?

Yes. Recycled metal is every bit as good as new metal, so it can be used over and over again. Recycling uses just a little of the energy needed to make new metal, so it saves lots of energy.

Cans are made from steel or aluminum. Both types are made from strips of metal formed into can shapes. They are coated with lacquer to stop them from rusting. Recycling aluminum costs less than recycling almost any other material.

One Small Fact
Two-thirds of cans on supermarket shelves are made of steel.

Millions of steel cans are recycled every year by using huge magnets to pull them out of household garbage.

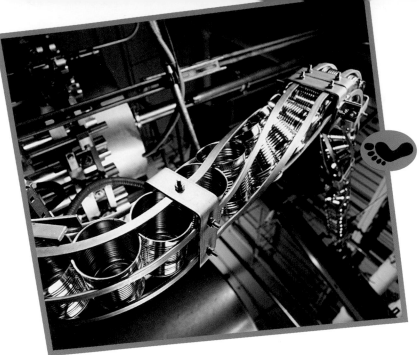

Recycling a steel can uses just a quarter of the energy needed to make a completely new one.

- Recycling one aluminum can saves enough energy to run a TV for three hours.

- Recycling one steel can saves enough energy to power a 60-watt light bulb for nearly four hours.

I Can Make a Difference

Not enough people recycle their cans. Can you think of ways to change this?

Does your school have a bin for recycled cans? If not, you could write to your city council to ask for one.

Why not have a collect-a-can week with a prize for the team that brings in the most cans to recycle?

You could also collect washed, used foil for recycling.

You Can Too!

American president George Bush gave one Californian school a special award for recycling. Every Friday, children brought in cans from home to recycle. The children asked their neighbors and local companies to help recycle too. They collected thousands of aluminum drink cans, soup cans, and plastic bottles and raised money for new playground equipment by selling them.

Can I Recycle Glass?

Glass can be recycled again and again. It is impossible to tell whether a glass bottle is newly made or recycled.

Empty glass jars and bottles are called cullet. They are sorted by color, such as green, brown, and clear. The glass is then crushed, mixed with raw materials, and melted at a high heat in a furnace. The melted glass is used to make new bottles or jars.

A tractor moves huge piles of crushed green glass at a glass recycling plant in West Virginia.

One Small Fact

Recycled glass uses 40% less energy than making new glass.

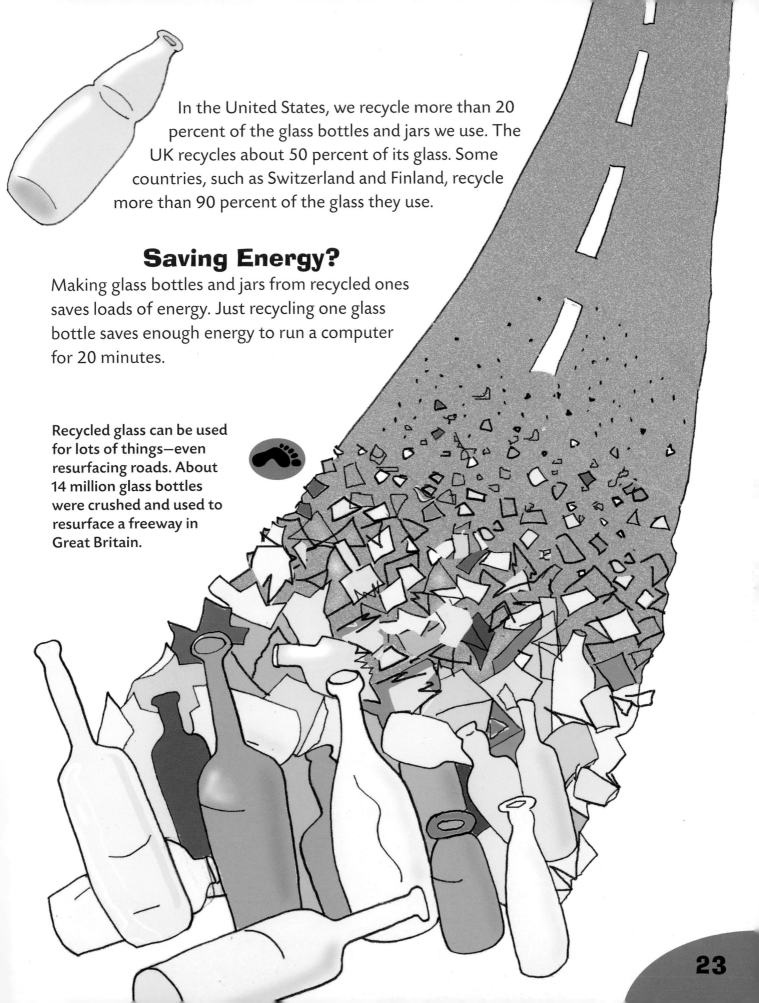

In the United States, we recycle more than 20 percent of the glass bottles and jars we use. The UK recycles about 50 percent of its glass. Some countries, such as Switzerland and Finland, recycle more than 90 percent of the glass they use.

Saving Energy?

Making glass bottles and jars from recycled ones saves loads of energy. Just recycling one glass bottle saves enough energy to run a computer for 20 minutes.

Recycled glass can be used for lots of things—even resurfacing roads. About 14 million glass bottles were crushed and used to resurface a freeway in Great Britain.

Can I Recycle Plastic?

Millions of plastic bottles are recycled every year. Most plastic is made from oil, and there are about 50 types of plastic.

Before they can be recycled, plastic bottles have to be sorted into the different types. Then the bottles are washed and broken into tiny flakes. When these have dried, they can be used to make new things.

One Small Fact

The city of San Francisco outlawed plastic bags in 2007.

I Can Make a Difference

If everyone in the U.S. stopped taking plastic bags in stores, there would be 100 billion fewer plastic bags thrown away every year. So why don't you start? Maybe your family and friends will follow your example.

What Can Be Made?

Lots of things can be made out of plastic bottles and other items.

- Soda pop and cooking oil bottles can be made into sleeping bags and parkas, new packaging, wall and floor coverings, and fleece clothing. It takes about 25 two-liter bottles to make one fleece jacket.

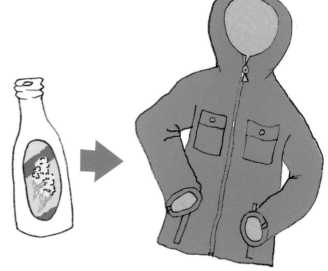

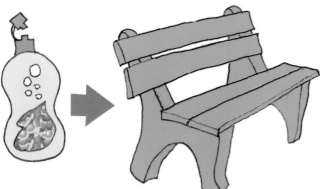

- Containers for fruit juice, dish soap, and fabric softener can be made into fences, park benches, and signposts. These bottles can also be refilled and used again and again.

- Mineral water, juice and shampoo bottles, as well as plastic food trays and plastic wrap, can be made into drainage pipes, electrical fittings, and clothing.

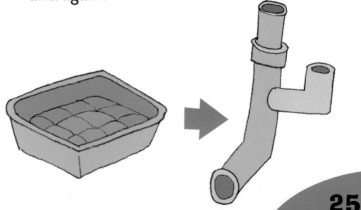

Can I Recycle Machines?

Lots of machines can be recycled or passed on to someone else when we are finished with them.

A cell phone should work for five years, but lots of people get a new one every year because they want the latest kind. Cell phones contain a chemical called cadmium. Each one contains enough cadmium to pollute 158,800 gallons (600,000 L) of water when it is thrown away. You can take old cell phones to charities, which can update and reuse them.

If cell phones are recycled, almost all of the materials used to make them can be used again.

One Small Fact

Americans throw away about 2 million tons (1.8 million t) of electrical items every year.

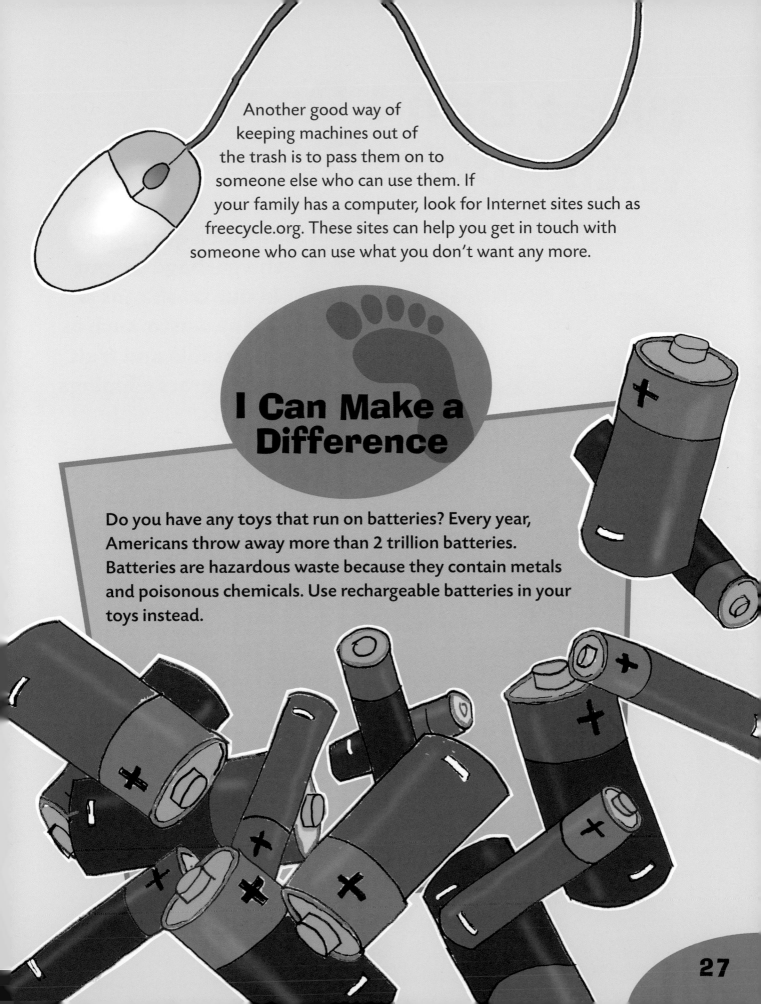

Another good way of keeping machines out of the trash is to pass them on to someone else who can use them. If your family has a computer, look for Internet sites such as freecycle.org. These sites can help you get in touch with someone who can use what you don't want any more.

I Can Make a Difference

Do you have any toys that run on batteries? Every year, Americans throw away more than 2 trillion batteries. Batteries are hazardous waste because they contain metals and poisonous chemicals. Use rechargeable batteries in your toys instead.

What Can I Do with Apple Cores?

Almost a quarter of the garbage we put in our trash cans is plant waste, such as vegetable and fruit peelings, grass clippings, and weeds.

When plant material is thrown away in a landfill site, it makes a harmful liquid called leachate. This is bad for water and soil. The best thing to do with plant waste is to put it all in a compost bin. It slowly rots down and can then be put on the garden to help plants grow. Always wash your hands after using the compost bin.

One Small Fact

It takes nine months to a year for your plant waste to turn into moist brown compost that can be put on the garden.

 Leftover fruits and vegetables are perfect for making compost.

✔ Put These in Your Compost Bin ✔

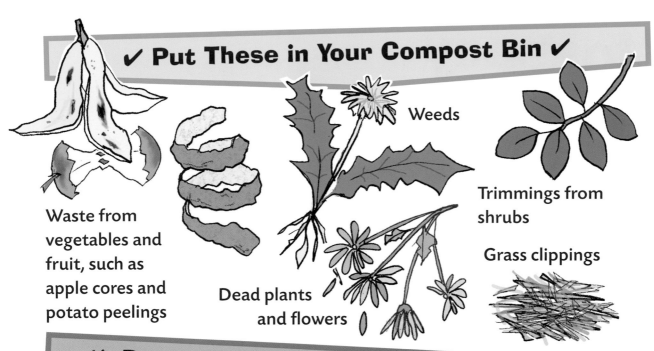

Waste from vegetables and fruit, such as apple cores and potato peelings

Weeds

Dead plants and flowers

Trimmings from shrubs

Grass clippings

✗ Don't Put These in Your Compost Bin ✗

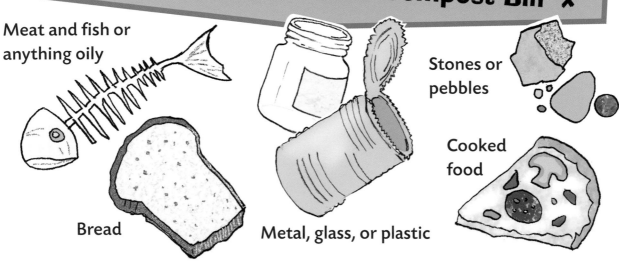

Meat and fish or anything oily

Bread

Metal, glass, or plastic

Stones or pebbles

Cooked food

Help your family or school start composting. You will need a compost bin with a lid and plastic buckets to collect the compost. Find an out-of-the-way corner and put your compost bin on grass or bare soil, not on concrete or blacktop.

I Can Make a Difference

Glossary

aluminum
A very light, silvery-gray metal. Most drink cans are made from aluminum.

biodegradable
Biodegradable garbage will rot away after awhile if it is thrown away. Fruit and grass clippings are biodegradable. Nonbiodegradable garbage, such as cans and plastic, will never rot.

compost
Rotted down plant and food waste that can be turned into plant food.

hazardous waste
Things people have thrown away which may contain dangerous chemicals, such as batteries or paint.

lacquer
A liquid that dries to make a smooth shiny coating and stops metal cans from rusting.

landfill site
A place where garbage is dumped and usually buried.

pulp
A soft, shapeless, wet pile of material. Paper is made from a pulp of fibers.

rechargeable battery
A rechargeable battery can be used again and again. When the battery runs out of energy, it can be placed into a recharger and refilled with energy.

recycle
To process old items such as glass, plastics, newspapers, and aluminum cans so the materials can be used to make new things.

Web Sites

http://www.eia.doe.gov/kids/energyfacts/saving/recycling/solidwaste/paperandglass.html
Facts about recycling paper and glass from the Energy Information Administration.

http://www.idahoptv.org/dialogue4kids/season6/garbage/facts.cfm
Facts about garbage, including what's in it, where it goes, and more.

http://www.dnr.state.wi.us/org/caer/ce/eek/earth/recycle/index.htm
Environmental Education for Kids offers stories, games, and information about recycling and composting.

http://www.epa.gov/recyclecity/
Interactive games and activities show you how "Dumptown" turned into "Recycle City."

http://www.ecokids.ca/pub/index.cfm
Canada's EcoKids Web site offers earth-saving ideas from other kids, homework help, and games and activities that teach about caring for the earth.

Index

Can I Use These Again? (see page 15)

Can be recycled at most recycling centers
newspapers   cereal boxes
glass bottles   plastic milk bottles
comics   cans
egg cartons

Can't be recycled
snack wrappers
empty felt-tipped pens
batteries (unless rechargeable)

Can be recycled, but not everywhere
orange juice cartons   yogurt cups

Can be recycled through charity shops or Web sites
televisions   toy cars   dolls

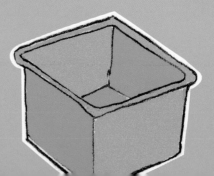